ENCYCLOPEDIA
of PRESIDENTS

Zachary Taylor

Twelfth President of the United States

By Zachary Kent

Consultant: Charles Abele, Ph.D.
Social Studies Instructor
Chicago Public School System

 CHILDRENS PRESS ®

CHICAGO

Zachary Taylor's home in Saint Matthews, Kentucky

Library of Congress Cataloging-in-Publication Data

Kent, Zachary.
   Zachary Taylor.

   (Encyclopedia of presidents)
   Includes index.
   Summary: A biography of "Old Rough and Ready" hero of
the Mexican War who became the twelfth president of the
United States.
   1.   Taylor, Zachary, 1784-1850—Juvenile literature.
2.   Presidents—United States—Biography—Juvenile
literature.   3.   Generals—United States—Biography—
Juvenile literature.   4.   United States—Politics and
government—1849-1853—Juvenile literature.   5.   United
States—History—War with Mexico, 1845-1848—Juvenile
literature.   [1.   Taylor, Zachary, 1784-1850.
2.   Presidents]   I.   Title.   II.   Series.
E422.K46   1988   973.6'3'0924   [B]   [92]   87-35774
ISBN 0-516-01352-1

Childrens Press®, Chicago
Copyright © 1988 by Regensteiner Publishing Enterprises, Inc.
All rights reserved. Published simultaneously in Canada.
Printed in the United States of America.
   8 9 10 R 97

Picture Acknowledgments

The Bettmann Archive—31, 33, 36, 50 (bottom),
63

Thomas Gilcrease Institute of American History
and Art—11

Historical Pictures Service—4, 5 (2 pictures), 6,
8, 9, 14, 17 (bottom), 19, 21 (top), 22, 23, 24,
27, 29 (bottom), 39, 40, 44, 50 (top), 56, 58
(right), 61 (2 pictures), 62, 65, 67, 70, 73
(2 pictures), 74, 75, 78, 82, 83 (2 pictures), 84,
87, 88, 89

Lester S. Levy Collection of Sheet Music, Special
Collections, Milton S. Eisenhower Library, Johns
Hopkins University—13, 68, 69

Courtesy Library of Congress—41, 47, 53
(2 pictures), 54, 55

North Wind Picture Archives—17 (top), 21
(bottom), 26, 29 (top), 35, 38, 49, 58 (left)

U.S. Bureau of Printing and Engraving—2

Cover design and illustration
by Steven Gaston Dobson

A medal issued to honor
Zachary Taylor for his bravery
in the Mexican War

President Zachary Taylor

Table of Contents

Chapter 1

"Old Rough and Ready"

Across the narrow mountain pass the American soldiers braced themselves to meet the attack. Before them, scrambling up from twisting gullies and deep ravines, thousands of Mexican infantrymen hurled themselves forward. Over ridges and across plateaus, waves of Mexican cavalrymen pointed their glittering lances and spurred their horses to charge. Since the start of America's territorial war with Mexico, United States troops commanded by General Zachary Taylor had made great advances into Mexico. September 23, 1847, however, found Taylor's men outnumbered four to one and struggling desperately for their lives near a ranch called Buena Vista.

Through the early morning hours of this second day of battle, some four thousand American volunteers crouched behind rocks and brush and feverishly fired their rifles. When Mexican lancers outflanked the left of the American line, one Indiana regiment panicked and fled in retreat. Other formations, exhausted and confused, also wavered and fell back.

President James K. Polk

Into this turmoil rode a sixty-two-year-old officer, with a fresh Mississippi regiment and a squadron of dragoons. Having secured his supply center a few miles to the north, Zachary Taylor had hurried back to Buena Vista to face the greatest challenge of his long military career.

Some national leaders doubted Taylor's fighting abilities. President James K. Polk confided to his diary, "General Taylor, I fear, is not the man for the command of the army. He is brave but he does not seem to have resources or grasp of mind enough to conduct such a campaign." The men who mattered, though, greatly admired their general. One young lieutenant, Ulysses S. Grant, later insisted, "No soldier could face either danger or responsibility more calmly than he. These are qualities more rarely found than genius or physical courage."

General Taylor at Buena Vista

Thirty-nine years of army service, at frontier outposts and in Indian wars, had earned Zachary Taylor the colorful nickname "Old Rough and Ready." The common soldiers knew he was not afraid to fight. Now the general rode to an exposed position at the center of the threatened line. Throwing one leg around the pommel of his saddle, he sat sideways on his favorite horse, Old Whitey. In this familiar posture, the thick-bodied, gray-haired man was recognized easily by all the troops nearby.

As bullets whistled about him, Taylor observed the situation. A staff officer, Major W. W. Bliss, returned from a fast inspection and woefully reported that the Americans were whipped. Calmly Taylor answered, "I know it, but the volunteers don't know it. Let them alone, we'll see what they do."

Another officer galloped up and suggested that the army retreat. With determination Taylor replied, "No, we will decide the battle here! I will never, alive, leave my wounded behind!"

Inspired by Taylor's firmness, American officers shifted their regiments to meet the encircling Mexicans. Colonel Jefferson Davis aligned his hardy Mississippi riflemen on the plateau near the Buena Vista ranch house. Indiana and Illinois regiments quickly joined them in support. Together these soldiers formed an enormous V with the open end facing the approaching enemy.

Dressed in handsome uniforms and with banners streaming, the lead brigade of Mexican cavalry confidently galloped into this trap.

Standing near General Taylor, Private Samuel Chamberlain watched the distant action breathlessly. "I heard General Taylor say, 'Steady boys! Steady for the honor of Old Mississippi!' and as the sharp crack of their rifles rang out and the leading horsemen went down, the General swung his old glazed cap and cried out, 'Well done, Jeff! Hurrah for Mississippi!' " In cross fire, the Americans shot scores of lancers from their horses, and in shock the surviving Mexican cavalrymen fled.

Having failed to break the left, the Mexicans next attacked the weakened center of the American line. Caught off balance and heavily outnumbered, gallant Illinoisans and Kentuckians swung their rifles like clubs and slashed at the enemy with their bowie knives. Overpowered at last, these Americans ran for the safety of nearby ravines.

A Mexican cavalryman

The Mexicans rushed into the gap left by these bloodied soldiers. At that crucial moment a battery of three cannons arrived from the right. Steadfastly General Taylor ordered Captain Braxton Bragg and his artillerymen to advance into the face of the enemy. "Maintain the position at every hazard," he ordered. Anxiously Bragg asked who would support him, and Taylor exclaimed, "Major Bliss and I will support you." Together the little band pushed ahead. As the charging Mexicans closed in, Taylor coolly watched the artillerymen load ammunition into the cannons. "What are you using, Captain, grape or canister?" he asked.

"Canister, General."

"Single or double?"

"Single."

"Well, double-shot your guns and give 'em hell, Bragg!"

At the last possible second, the cannons exploded with great roars and flashes of fire. Like huge shotgun blasts, fragmenting loads of double-canister ammunition mowed the enemy down. The Mexican force was staggered. A second salvo and then a third drove them back in dazed horror. Soon American infantry regiments rushed to the scene to give Bragg the real support he needed.

Throughout the afternoon the battle raged. The Mexicans rallied and attacked again. The crackle of gunfire and the screams of the wounded echoed through the mountain gorge. Great clouds of dust and smoke billowed up and filled the sky. Two shots ripped through General Taylor's uniform coat, but he remained unscratched. Staying where the fight was thickest, his calm orders and lively encouragement gave his men continued faith and energy.

In late afternoon a rainstorm stopped the fighting for a time, and when darkness arrived at last the battlefield fell quiet. After a wet and worrisome night, the Americans awoke to discover the Mexican army was gone. Joyfully, General Taylor and General John E. Wool embraced and laughed aloud. The battle of Buena Vista was over, and against great odds Taylor's men had won.

As news of the astounding victory traveled northward, the general's political enemies claimed that he was merely lucky. Most Americans, however, cheered his latest battlefield success. Already admired for his honesty and simple style, Old Rough and Ready now became a legend. Senator Daniel Webster wrote, "Gen. Taylor's popularity seems to spread like wild fire." In the next two years it would sweep Zachary Taylor into the White House.

Opposite page: Cover of an
1848 Taylor campaign song

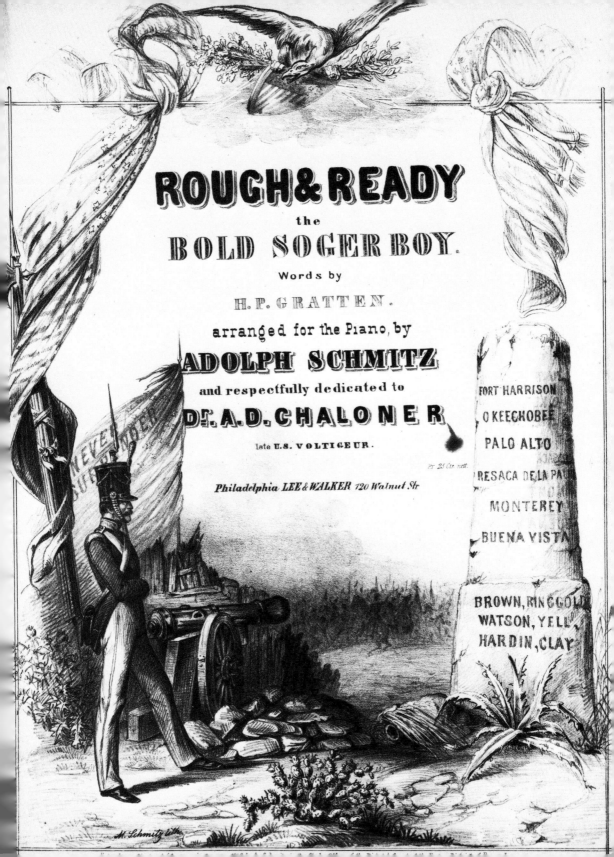

Chapter 2

The Making of a Soldier

It seems fitting that Zachary Taylor, the future border soldier, began his life on the move, headed toward the wilderness. He was born in a rough-hewn plantation cabin on November 24, 1784, in Orange County, Virginia, near the town of Barboursville. His parents, Lieutenant Colonel Richard Taylor and Sarah Strother Taylor, were both members of old and respected Virginia families. Yet the autumn of 1784 found the Taylors uprooted and traveling toward Kentucky. For his services in the American Revolution, Colonel Taylor had been rewarded with six thousand acres of western land, and he was determined to settle on this new frontier.

After stopping at a relative's farm for the birth of their third child, Zachary, the Taylors continued on in the spring of 1785 to cross the Appalachian Mountains. Their hard journey brought them at last to Beargrass Creek near Louisville. Surely young Zach's first memories were of the family's crude log cabin and of the simple farm his father cut from the forest. Although it was beautiful country, western Kentucky was still very wild. A visitor at the Taylor homestead remembered, "Here we were saluted every night with the howling of wolves."

Opposite page: Young Zachary Taylor
learns frontiersman's skills.

15

Through these early years of settlement, marauding Indians often lurked about the woods. Fear of Indian attack kept settlers on constant alert. The sound of gunfire brought Kentuckians rushing to the aid of neighbors, and at night the Taylors barricaded their doors and windows to protect themselves.

On one occasion, some neighborhood boys were found murdered and scalped near the spot where Zach and his brothers had split up with them earlier in the day. The dangers and difficulties of frontier life helped form the young man's character.

Little is known of Zach's early education. Colonel Taylor hired tutors for his children when he could, and for a time a wandering Connecticut schoolteacher named Elisha Ayer taught Zach reading, writing, and arithmetic. Ayer judged his young student, "quick in learning, and . . . patient in study." As a teenager Zach sometimes attended a neighborhood school taught by Kean O'Hara, a respected local scholar. It is easy to imagine that Zach's educated parents read with him and taught him lessons in the evenings while sitting before a crackling fire. Yet the letters Zach wrote in manhood show him to be a poor speller.

The truth was that a formal education in frontier Kentucky was not considered very important. There was too much farm work to be done, and every day Zach performed his share of chores. With eight brothers and sisters, the boy never lacked for companionship. Together the family worked and watched the farm grow into a prosperous tobacco plantation.

Right: A pioneer woman defends her household against invasion by a band of Indians.

Below: A scene in the Blue Ridge Mountains of Kentucky in the 1800s.

For amusement Zach often rode horseback on backwoods trails. Some days he loaded a rifle and stalked the forest for deer and raccoon. At other times he sat fishing on the nearby banks of the Ohio River. At the age of seventeen Zach proved his strength and hardiness by plunging into the icy waters of that wide river and swimming from Kentucky across to Indiana and back.

Long before he reached the age of twenty, Zachary Taylor showed many traits that would remain with him all his life. Neighbors and family recalled that he had a fine memory and a streak of stubbornness. He was kindhearted and friendly, and in his actions robust and energetic.

Throughout his childhood Zach enjoyed playing at soldier. He thrilled at leading his playmates in make-believe charges. When his father told stories of revolutionary battles, Zach listened with excitement and curious attention. It was not surprising, then, that at the age of twenty-three he expressed a desire to join the army.

In applying for a military appointment, the Taylor family connections came in handy. Zachary Taylor's second cousin, James Madison, had held the office of secretary of state in 1808 and would soon be elected fourth president of the United States. In a letter of recommendation, James Taylor, another cousin, told Madison, "I think Z. Taylor will make a valuable Officer. He is much Esteemed by all who are acquainted with him. He appears to possess a great deal of that frank bluntness and firmness which his father is so remarkable for." Madison and the War Department agreed, and on May 3, 1808, Taylor received a commission as first lieutenant of infantry.

Margaret Smith Taylor, Zachary's wife

Dressed in a uniform of single-breasted blue coat, blue pantaloons, and stiff leather cap, the young officer took up duties in Kentucky and later in New Orleans. Taylor learned about the army firsthand and not out of textbooks. In payment for his military services he received two meals a day and thirty dollars a month.

On June 21, 1810, at the age of twenty-five, First Lieutenant Taylor married twenty-one-year-old Margaret Mackall Smith at her brother-in-law's home near Louisville. Born in Maryland, the refined and lovely bride was the daughter of a successful planter. The devoted newlyweds enjoyed many years of marriage. As often as possible when her husband was transferred to a new post, Mrs. Taylor packed up and came with him. Together they would have five daughters and a son.

Along with a promotion to captain in the spring of 1811, Taylor received orders to take command of Fort Knox at Vincennes in the Indiana Territory. The fort badly needed repairs, so Taylor quickly put his men to work. Within two weeks, military governor William Henry Harrison happily wrote to the War Department: "In the short time he has been a commander he has rendered the Garrison defensible—before his arrival it resembled anything . . . but a place of defense."

America's northwestern frontier required just such tough and resourceful officers in the summer of 1812. After years of strained relations, the United States declared war on Great Britain on June 19, 1812. As the fighting commenced, British troops marched down from Canada.

Joined by Indian allies, the British captured one American fort after another. Transferred to the command of Fort Harrison farther up the Wabash River, Captain Taylor hurried there and prepared to defend the place. Deep within enemy territory, just fifty soldiers occupied the small log stockade. Most of these exhausted men lay in their barracks beds, stricken with fever.

On the night of September 4, 1812, 450 Indians, led by the fierce Shawnee chief Tecumseh, crept through the woods and surrounded the fort. "About eleven o'clock," Taylor later reported, "I was awakened by the firing of one of the sentinels. I sprung up, ran out, and ordered the men to their posts, when my orderly sergeant . . . called out that the Indians had fired the lower block-house."

Right: Shawnee
chief Tecumseh

Below: The British
capture and burn
Washington, D.C.,
during the War of
1812.

Zachary Taylor defending Fort Harrison against Tecumseh's attack

The burning wood spit sparks, flames lit up the sky. As the fire raged, the screaming Indians showered the fort with arrows and gunfire. Taylor roused his men and called for buckets of water. "As that block-house adjoined the barracks that made up part of the fortification," he remembered, "most of the men immediately gave themselves up for lost. . . . But my presence of mind did not for the moment forsake me. I saw by throwing off part of the roof . . . the whole row of buildings might be saved."

With desperate energy Taylor and his men yanked down the roof and doused the blaze. Although a few soldiers were killed and others fell wounded, through the night the little garrison kept the Indians from entering the fort.

Fort Harrison a year after the Indian attack

With relief Taylor reported, "The Indians suffered smartly. . . . They continued with us until the next morning, but made no further attempt on the fort, nor have we seen anything more of them since."

News of Taylor's daring and fortitude spread quickly. Acting Indiana governor John Gibson proudly referred to "the brave defense made by Captain Taylor at Ft. Harrison" as "one bright ray amid the gloom of incompetency which has been shown in so many places." During the next year Taylor took part in several smaller expeditions against the British and the Indians, but people best remembered his heroic stand at Fort Harrison. In recognition for his service that day, the U.S. Army promoted Taylor to the brevet, or temporary, rank of major.

An engraving of Zachary Taylor

Chapter 3

On the Frontier Line

A year before the December 1814 signing of the Treaty of Ghent, which ended the War of 1812, United States troops had pushed the British out of the American Northwest. With the reorganization of the peacetime army, Taylor believed there was no place for him. In 1815 he resigned and set up a farm near Louisville. Although he loved farming, his love for the military life soon proved stronger. In May 1816 Taylor accepted reappointment in the army, and for the next thirty-three years he would serve as a U.S. soldier.

Major Taylor's first assignment took him by boat to Fort Howard, where Green Bay, Wisconsin, stands today. There he endured two icy winters while protecting the region's fur trappers. Promoted to lieutenant colonel in 1819, he next received orders to report to the southwest frontier of Louisiana. His wife and young family packed their trunks and joined him. Taylor greatly admired the Louisiana countryside and considered establishing a plantation for himself. Louisiana's hot and swampy climate, however, inflicted tragedy on the Taylor family. At Bayou Sara near Baton Rouge, Taylor's little daughters Octavia and Margaret died of fever in 1820.

Slaves picking cotton on a plantation in the South

Deeply saddened, Taylor still insisted on continuing his southwestern border duties. At the head of his regiment, he supervised the chopping of a difficult two-hundred-mile wilderness road across Louisiana. Later his men built and garrisoned Fort Jesup along the territory's westernmost border. Before leaving for duty in Kentucky in 1824, Taylor bought a five-hundred-acre cotton plantation forty miles north of Baton Rouge. To oversee this farm and its twenty-two black slaves, Taylor found "a first rate young man as a manager, who will have as much done as I wish my hands to do, & will have every thing as well attended to as if I was personally present." For the next dozen years

The interior of Fort Snelling

Taylor ran the business of his farm almost entirely by sending written instructions through the mail.

A reshuffling of troops by the War Department in the summer of 1828 sent the forty-three-year-old officer traveling from one end of the Mississippi River to the other. As the new commandant of Fort Snelling (present-day Minneapolis, Minnesota) Taylor settled into large, comfortable quarters. This fort was built with thick walls of stone. When Taylor next was transferred to Fort Crawford at Prairie de Chien in the Michigan Territory (now Wisconsin), he watched his soldiers rebuild decayed wooden buildings there with stone as well.

Training the soldiers to defend these forts occupied Taylor much of the time. One day at Fort Crawford the lieutenant colonel watched the garrison assemble on "dress parade." One new German recruit, not understanding orders, stood improperly on line. "Col. Taylor remarked this," remembered Corporal John N. Fonda, "and thinking it a willful neglect on the soldier's part, walked up to him . . . got hold of his ears and shook the fellow severely. This treatment was called 'wooling,' a favorite mode of punishment with Taylor, but the German not knowing . . . why it was inflicted on him had no sooner got his head free than drawing back he struck Taylor a blow that felled him to the ground like a dog. This was mutiny and the officers and guard would have cut him down, if Taylor had not rose up and said, 'let that man alone, he will make a good soldier.' " Bluff and brawny, Taylor took an honest and practical interest in his troops.

Not long after Taylor's promotion to full colonel in April 1832, an Indian war erupted in the northwest corner of Illinois. For years homesteaders had encroached upon the lands of the Sac and Fox Indians in that portion of the state. Forced across the Mississippi River into Iowa, the Sac and Fox longed to return to their homeland beside the Rock River. Finally, a Sac chief named Black Hawk gathered together about five hundred warriors. With their women, children, and baggage, these Indians crossed back into the Rock River region. Horrified white squatters tried to drive out Black Hawk's group. In response, Sac braves attacked and murdered settlers and threw the area into panic.

Above: Chief Black Hawk

Right: Abraham Lincoln, who was elected captain of his group of Illinois militiamen during the Black Hawk wars. A story is told that Lincoln defended an Indian against angry settlers and soldiers.

As the massacre and scalping continued, General Henry Atkinson hurriedly assembled a force of regular troops and Illinois militia. Returning north from a Louisiana visit, Zachary Taylor took command of part of this army. "We set out in pursuit of the enemy," Taylor later recalled. "But Black Hawk and his warriors proved difficult to catch." Rather than fight in open battle, Black Hawk and his men retreated beyond the Rock River. The undisciplined Illinois militiamen in Taylor's force suddenly refused to pursue the enemy into this unsettled area. With his regular troops to support him, Colonel Taylor confronted these mutineers. "Gentlemen and fellow-citizens," he sternly warned them, "the word has been passed onto me from Washington, to follow Black Hawk, and to take you with me as soldiers. I mean to do both." Realizing the forty-seven-year-old army veteran meant business, the militiamen unhappily climbed aboard waiting flatboats and crossed the Rock River.

On horseback and on foot, through the sweltering summer months, Taylor and his army chased Black Hawk's renegades. Across Illinois and into the Wisconsin wilderness Taylor pushed ahead. Some soldiers fell beside the forest trails sick or exhausted, but the army continued forward. During a full month's march the colonel remembered the suffering of his men "in wading daily swamps & marshes & passing over a number of hills that in Europe would be termed mountains which before had never been passed by a white man even a trader, much less an army."

Finally on August 2, 1832, these soldiers caught up with Black Hawk's band as they tried to escape across the

Jefferson Davis, president of the Confederacy

Mississippi River. At the battle of Bad Axe, bullets ripped through the Wisconsin trees amid bloody war cries. When the smoke cleared, some one hundred Indians and twenty-seven militiamen lay dead or wounded. In the following days, many Indians surrendered, including the famous Sac chieftain himself. Many Indians were massacred even after attempting to surrender. Taylor had broken the back of Black Hawk's war.

Two soldiers who took part in the conflict of that summer would one day oppose each other during America's Civil War. Illinois volunteer Abraham Lincoln finished his service in July and returned to his clerking job in New Salem, little dreaming he would one day be president of the United States. West Point graduate and future president of the Confederate States of America, Lieutenant Jefferson Davis remained on active duty. He would soon take a personal interest in Colonel Taylor's family.

With calm restored to the northwest region, Colonel Taylor returned to Fort Crawford. This fortress, with its growing community of settlers, served as his headquarters during the next five years. The military administration of the frontier district, road building, and the training of peacekeeping troops occupied the colonel much of the time.

But Taylor also managed to enjoy a certain degree of social life. Sutlers (civilian merchants) had set up shop at Fort Crawford and were selling all kinds of general merchandise. Soldiers sometimes transformed a barracks room into a theater where they performed plays. The post possessed a library and a school that soldiers' children attended. Officers and civilians who were invited to dine at the commandant's table came away impressed by the pleasant conversation of Colonel Taylor, Mrs. Taylor, and the daughters who lived with them.

In 1829 Taylor's eldest daughter, Ann, had married an army surgeon. Now at Fort Crawford, Lieutenant Jefferson Davis began courting Taylor's second daughter, Sarah. At first the colonel strongly objected. He wanted something better than an unsettled army life for his daughter. The love shared by the two young people proved too strong, however.

With her parents' reluctant consent, Sarah Knox Taylor married Jefferson Davis on June 17, 1835. Sadly, the Taylors never saw their daughter again. Following the wedding, Davis took his bride to Mississippi where he intended to establish a plantation. Three months later she died, a victim of malarial fever.

Jefferson Davis with his wife, Sarah Knox Taylor

Only time could heal the wound of this loss, and before long another Indian war fully occupied Taylor's attention. For years Florida's Seminole tribes had resisted white settlement in their territory. Responding to unfair treaties and encroaching homesteaders, these natives returned to the warpath in 1835. To help defeat this uprising, known as the Second Seminole War, Colonel Taylor received notice to bring his regiment south in 1837. Placed in command of one thousand men, Taylor grimly marched eastward from Tampa Bay intending to attack the Seminole warriors "wherever found and in whatever numbers."

The long hunt for the enemy carried Taylor and his army through the worst possible terrain. For days these soldiers plunged across open marshes, through mosquito-infested swamps, and over rising hammocks—fertile, elevated Florida terrain—dense with cypress trees and sharp saw grass. Finally, with the help of Indian guides, Taylor came upon the Seminoles on December 25, 1837, at Lake Okeechobee. Beyond a broad swamp some seven hundred warriors of the Mikasuki tribe crouched among the brush and trees of a long hammock.

Forming a battle line, Colonel Taylor waded forward with his men through knee-deep mud. As they neared the hammock the Seminoles poured forth a hail of gunfire. Some soldiers panicked and ran for safety, but most refused to budge. Returning shot for shot, by the end of three hours these tough soldiers broke through the Indians' line. With loud shouts the troops chased the retreating natives until after nightfall.

On the Okeechobee battleground, Taylor's men buried the dead and placed the wounded on roughly made stretchers. Although the bodies of only fourteen Indians were found, the Americans suffered 138 men killed or wounded. "The victory was dearly purchased," admitted Taylor.

Still he had reason to be proud. "This column," he soon reported, "in six weeks, penetrated one hundred and fifty miles into the enemy's country, opened roads, and constructed bridges and causeways . . . established two depots, and the necessary defenses for the same, and finally overtook and beat the enemy in his strongest position."

Seminole Indians under the leadership of their chief, Osceola, attack Fort King in Florida.

During the following months many disheartened and hungry Seminoles stepped from the swamps and surrendered. The fight at Okeechobee had shown them they were powerless to defeat the Americans. Highly commended for his Florida services, Taylor received a promotion from the War Department to brevet brigadier general in 1838. Perhaps more important, he came out of the Florida swamp with a nickname. Because the sturdy old officer preferred plain, almost rough clothes and was always ready to endure the hardships of his men or lead them in a fight, admiring soldiers took to calling Taylor "Old Rough and Ready."

Major General Zachary Taylor

Chapter 4

The Coming War with Mexico

After the difficulties of the Florida campaign, General Taylor requested a transfer to command the army's Second Military Department in 1841. This district encompassed parts of Louisiana, Arkansas, and the Oklahoma territory. Taylor chose to make his headquarters at Fort Smith, Arkansas. During the next three years he built new forts on the Red River and elsewhere. Inspection tours of these border forts kept Taylor in the saddle for weeks at a time. Being stationed in the Southwest, however, gave Taylor an opportunity to attend to his private affairs. In December 1841 the general bought a second river plantation for $95,000. Farther north of Baton Rouge, Taylor's Cypress Grove plantation stretched over 2,100 acres in Jefferson County, Mississippi.

In purchasing the Baton Rouge estate, Taylor obtained a large number of black slaves. It is believed that at the time of his death he owned as many as 127 slaves. These workers planted the long cotton rows and at harvest time picked the fluffy cotton bolls. They tended vegetable gardens, raised livestock, and sometimes cut wood, hauled it to the river, and sold it to passing steamboats for fuel.

Slaves working the cotton fields on a plantation in the South

A careful businessman and a sympathetic master, General Taylor instructed his overseer to treat his servants well. An Englishwoman visiting at Cypress Grove one winter observed that Taylor's slaves were all "well fed, comfortably clothed, and kindly cared for." The men walked about in warm flannel trousers, and their wives wore dresses of clean white calico, "while almost all had woolen shawls." Taylor demanded that sick field hands be allowed to rest until they regained their health, and on at least one occasion he wrote to his overseer: "Distribute . . . five hundred dollars . . . among the servants at Christmas . . . in such a way as you think they deserve by their good conduct."

Texan troops assembling in Houston in 1844

After a lifetime in the army, a peaceful retirement would have been welcome to Zachary Taylor. But Old Rough and Ready refused to turn his back when duty beckoned him once again. The War Department called the troops gathering in southwestern Louisiana a "corps of observation." However, upon his arrival at Fort Jesup in June 1844, General Taylor was instructed to keep his new command "in readiness for service at any moment."

Just across the Sabine River stretched the foreign Republic of Texas. Hard-fought battles such as those at the Alamo and San Jacinto had won American settlers in Texas their independence from Mexico in 1836. Texans had wished to join the Union then, but the slavery question presented many problems. In 1844, when annexation negotiations finally began in Washington, D.C., the embittered Mexicans threatened war.

Ulysses S. Grant as a lieutenant in the Mexican War in 1846

The barracks at Fort Jesup were too small to house the entire army. Therefore, the Third and Fourth Infantry regiments built a camp for themselves nearby. Row upon row of tents marked this pleasant place, which the soldiers named Camp Salubrity. Lieutenant Ulysses S. Grant, fresh out of West Point, later vividly remembered that the camp "was on a high, sandy, pine ridge, with spring branches in the Valley, in front and rear. The springs furnished an abundance of cool, pure water. . . ."

Grant and his fellow soldiers grew used to seeing their commander about the camp. Standing five feet eight inches in height, Taylor was a broad-chested, stocky man. Troops observed that the general's bowed legs were so short that he often required help climbing into the saddle. With squinting gray eyes, a weathered face, and a large head of curly gray hair, Taylor appeared fierce enough. His casual camp behavior, however, often confused people.

Taylor's army assembles near Corpus Christi, Texas, in October 1845.

Unlike most high-ranking officers, Taylor preferred to do without fancy uniforms. For comfort his usual camp clothing consisted of baggy cotton pants, a long plain linen coat, and a wide-brimmed straw hat to shade him from the sun. With the general dressed in this outfit, new arrivals in camp often failed to recognize him. "He looks more like an old farmer going to market with eggs to sell," remarked one surprised Indiana captain.

While a Texas convention met in the spring of 1845 to consider annexation, Mexico increased its threats of war. Couriers rushed dispatches from Secretary of State James Buchanan to General Taylor. "Texas must be protected from hostile invasion," he instructed. Taylor was ordered to put his forces "into a position where they may most promptly and efficiently act in defense of Texas." So the general moved his army to the mouth of the Nueces River, which Mexico claimed was the Texas border.

Private Barna Upton witnessed the activity at Fort Jesup on July 3, 1845. "Everything is bustling, packing, and preparing for the march," he revealed. "All are eager to start, animation and enthusiasm is the order of the day." Over land and by boat, the army traveled to the village of Corpus Christi, Texas. In this flat country of thorny cactus and thick chaparral, four thousand troops—half of the entire United States Army—assembled in September 1845. The men pitched tents and built fires and marveled at their strange surroundings. "There are lots of rattlesnakes here," exclaimed Private Upton, "and the lightning bugs are six times as large here as at the North." Through the winter months the men huddled miserably as Gulf Coast storms swept the camp with wet, cold weather.

On December 29, 1845, Texas officially became the twenty-eighth state to join the Union. Taylor's soldiers greeted the news with cheers and celebrations. They realized, though, that war with Mexico now loomed closer than ever. With the addition of Texas, the United States claimed as its foreign boundary the banks of the Rio Grande. The Mexicans refused to accept that line, and all peaceful attempts to reach an understanding failed.

To enforce its territorial claim, the United States ordered General Taylor to proceed to the Rio Grande. On March 8, 1846, Taylor's army once more broke camp. Cavalrymen trotted forward on horseback, teams of oxen drew cannon and supply wagons, and infantry regiments followed on foot as the force started its 180-mile journey southward. Warnings that a huge Mexican army intended to stop his progress failed to frighten Taylor. Lieutenant

George G. Meade overheard the general bluntly announce that even "if there were fifty thousand Mexicans he would try his best to get there."

After a long, hot march, late in the morning of March 28 the American army reached the waters of the Rio Grande. Just across the river, a large Mexican army had fortified itself in the town of Matamoros. From the distant adobe rooftops, Mexican officers watched Taylor's soldiers construct a stockade later called Fort Brown, where Brownsville, Texas, stands today.

For two weeks both armies strengthened their defenses and glared at one another across the river. Then on April 12 Mexican General Pedro de Ampudia sent the Americans a stern warning: "I require you in all form, and at latest in . . . twenty-four hours, to break up your camp and retire to the other bank of the Nueces River. . . . If you insist in remaining . . . arms and arms alone, must decide the question." General Taylor sent back a firm answer: "The instructions under which I am acting will not permit me to retrograde from the position I now occupy."

The smoldering powder keg of war finally exploded on April 24. On that day several hundred Mexican soldiers ambushed an American scouting party on the north side of the Rio Grande. Captain Seth Thornton and his sixty-three dragoons fiercely defended themselves until they were overpowered and all were killed or captured. When word of the fight reached General Taylor, he quickly sent a dispatch to President James K. Polk. "Hostilities," he bluntly stated, "may now be considered as commenced."

Chapter 5

"Our Victory Has Been Decisive"

"To arms! To arms!" trumpeted the New Orleans *Daily Delta* when word of the Mexican attack arrived in that city, "in the maintenance of our national honor! in support of our undoubted rights! in revenge for our slaughtered countrymen—to arms!" In New York City, crowds packed the streets with placards reading "Mexico or Death!" and "Ho, for the halls of Montezuma!" On May 11, President Polk hastened a message to Congress urging that war be declared, saying that Mexican troops had invaded American territory and shed American blood on American soil.

On May 1, Taylor had set two thousand of his men on a twenty-six-mile march to the Gulf of Mexico. Arriving at Point Isabel, soldiers secured the American supply center there and collected two hundred wagons of needed ammunition and food. At dawn on May 3, while still encamped on the coast, Lieutenant Samuel French was shaken awake by the "boom! boom! of distant cannon." Lieutenant E. Kirby Smith remembered the sudden sound as a "rumbling noise like distant thunder." The Mexicans were bombarding the five-hundred-man garrison Taylor had left to defend Fort Brown. Determined to rescue the besieged fort, Taylor finished loading his supply wagons and ordered his men on the road again. To Washington, D.C., the general wrote, "If the enemy oppose my march, in whatever force, I shall fight him."

On May 7 the wagons of Taylor's army rolled back toward Fort Brown and the tramping feet of his two thousand men filled the muggy air with dust. The march stopped abruptly twelve miles from Fort Brown on the following afternoon. Blocking the road half a mile ahead waited a Mexican army well over twice the size of Taylor's. Gun barrels and bayonets glistened in the sunlight along a Mexican battle line that stretched a mile across a prairie of tall grass. Dotted with muddy waterholes and backed by a thicket of tall trees, the place was called Palo Alto.

True to his word, General Taylor prepared his men to fight. Infantry regiments fell into line and ox teams pulled artillery pieces into position. As Taylor sat on Old Whitey, calmly chewing tobacco, his young soldiers waited nervously for their final orders. Lieutenant French remembered that "hearts beat, pulses kept time, and knees trembled and would not be still."

Slowly the Americans advanced, and the Mexican cannon suddenly opened fire. "Now for the first time I found myself in battle," exclaimed Private Upton. The marksmanship of the Mexican artillerymen, however, proved to be very poor. The cannonballs, remarked Upton, "were constantly hissing over our heads or mowing their way through the tall grass, and it was astonishing how few struck our ranks."

The Battle of Palo Alto on May 8, 1846

The answering American cannon proved much more accurate and deadly. Firing grapeshot and exploding shells instead of solid cannonballs, Taylor's artillery fire tore into the charging enemy. Later, walking over the field, army surgeon Madison Mills observed "heads and limbs severed from their bodies and trunks strewed about in awful confusion."

A Mexican cavalry charge tried to turn the American right flank. "Here they come!" shouted men of the Fifth Infantry Regiment. Several precise rifle volleys and the quick support of a battery of "flying artillery" put a bloody halt to that attack. The rapidly shifting artillery batteries proved Taylor's greatest weapon. Throughout the afternoon the general relied on their speed and effectiveness. As the battle raged, Lieutenant Smith heard "some twenty pieces of artillery thundering from right to left [and] the tramping horses and the wild cheering of men."

At one point a cannon flame set the prairie on fire. The burning grass and thick smoke halted the battle for an hour. When the fighting resumed it was clear that the Mexicans were weakening. As the sun went down, the enemy withdrew from the field. The battle of Palo Alto left 55 Americans killed, wounded, or missing. The Mexican casualties of more than 250 men clearly showed that the Americans had won this cannon duel.

Through the night Taylor saw that his wounded men received medical treatment. On the morning of May 9, scouts brought in reports of a new Mexican battle line. A few miles farther up the road the enemy had entrenched along the banks of an old river bed. This sunken, twisting ravine contained narrow ponds of stagnant water, matted thorny brush, and thickets of small trees. Called Resaca de la Palma, it gave the Mexicans a strong defensive position.

A group of officers cautioned General Taylor to dig in and await reinforcements. After considering their advice the old soldier announced, "I shall go to Fort Brown or stay in my shoes" (meaning he would go to the aid of the fort or die fighting with his boots on). To the sound of bugle calls and drum beats, Taylor's army marched to Resaca de la Palma.

"A universal rattle of musketry and thunder of cannon soon commenced," recalled Private Upton. "The whole chaparral was raked by the enemy's grapeshot, cannon and musket balls." In an attempt to silence a Mexican battery that blocked the road, Taylor threw artillery lieutenant Randolph Ridgely forward with his gun crews. With difficulty American platoons edged ahead through the

The charge of Captain May's cavalry, from a print made at the time

prickly chaparral. Encountering Mexicans, these small units engaged in bloody, scattered, hand-to-hand fights. A desperate Mexican cavalry attack failed to dislodge Ridgely's guns. Grapeshot and canister shells left the ground littered with Mexican horsemen. Still the Americans could not break the strong enemy line.

Turning in his saddle, General Taylor ordered Captain Charles May to capture the Mexicans' most important cannon pieces. "I will do it, sir," answered the cavalry officer. "Men, follow me!" he shouted to his squadron of dragoons. The horsemen galloped forward until they reached Ridgely's artillery.

"Hello, Ridgely," yelled Captain May. "Where is that battery? I am ordered to charge it."

"Hold on, Charley," answered the lieutenant, " 'till I draw their fire and you will see where they are."

**Two different artists' versions of Captain May's charge
through the Mexican artillery line at Resaca de la Palma**

In another instant the opposing cannoneers fired their guns at one another. Guided by the smoke and gunflashes, Captain May charged the Mexican artillery before it could be reloaded. Slashing sabers cut down the Mexican soldiers as they ran away. Returning to the American lines, May presented Taylor with an important prisoner, General Díaz de la Vega, the Mexican field commander.

The tide of the battle had turned, but the combat raged for two more hours. "The enemy . . . fought like devils," exclaimed Lieutenant Smith. Finally, in the afternoon, the enemy resistance collapsed. The routed Mexicans crashed in confusion through the underbrush and fled for the Rio Grande. Many frightened Mexican soldiers threw themselves into the water and drowned trying to swim to safety. Behind them on the Resaca de la Palma battlefield they abandoned their wounded comrades, pack mules, baggage, and guns. The encounter cost the Mexicans over 500 men, compared with American losses of 122.

Great cheers rose up from the Fort Brown garrison as they spotted American soldiers marching on the road. "Our victory has been decisive," reported General Taylor, and ". . . the causes . . . are doubtless to be found in the superior quality of our officers and men." Completely stunned by the disaster, captured General de la Vega admitted, "If I had had with me yesterday $100,000 in silver, I would have bet the whole of it that no 10,000 men on earth could drive us from our position." Writing to his family, Private Upton described the battle in more simple terms: "Well, we did have a fight and a pretty tall one for these days."

On May 18 the beaten Mexicans abandoned Matamoros. Crossing the muddy waters of the Rio Grande, Taylor's troops triumphantly entered the Mexican town. In the United States, news of the two victories filled Americans with joy and made Taylor a national hero. People admired the fearless old veteran who had overcome the odds. Congress immediately promoted him and sent its official thanks "to Major General Zachary Taylor, . . . his officers and men, for the fortitude, skill, enterprise, and courage, which have distinguished the recent brilliant operations on the Rio Grande."

The promise of success so early in the war caused regiments of excited militiamen to hurry south to join Taylor's army. With these volunteers Taylor was told to continue his march into Mexico.

Privately the crusty old soldier revealed, "I want nothing more than to see this campaign finished & the war brought to a speedy and honorable close." With loyalty and energy, however, he prepared his growing army for continued battle.

The job of supplying the thousands of volunteers who poured into Matamoros quickly tested General Taylor's patience. The training of the inexperienced militiamen also required time. Drill instructors marched regiments across Matamoros fields and held target practice to improve marksmanship. Tough discipline taught wild soldiers to obey military regulations. Taylor was glad to note that one of the better volunteer regiments was the First Mississippi Rifles, commanded by his son-in-law Colonel Jefferson Davis.

Above: The Battle of Cerro Gordo
Below: The bombardment of Vera Cruz

Scene in Vera Cruz during the bombardment

Finally in July the general set his army in motion. By boat and by land he moved the bulk of his troops up the Rio Grande to the Mexican village of Camargo. From there Taylor intended to strike inland at the stronghold city of Monterrey. Eagerly the troops awaited the beginning of the campaign. Lieutenant Smith wrote home: "We are all busily engaged in making our preparations for crossing the mountains. . . . Nor will we be disappointed in soon engaging [the Mexicans] at Monteray, for the Gen. sitts [sic] cross-legged in his tent, as grum as old bear—sure indication of the coming storm."

54

An engraving of General Zachary Taylor

BUENA
VISTA

Engd by W. Wellstood

Chapter 6

Final Battles of the
Mexican War

At the end of August, Taylor's army broke camp and headed south into the Sierra Madre Mountains. A shortage of supply wagons and pack mules, however, forced Taylor to leave behind more than half of his troops. With an army of only 6,600 soldiers, the general journeyed one hundred miles across deserts and over mountain trails. Finally, on the misty morning of September 19, the army's advance guard rode out of the mountains and approached the city of Monterrey.

Rising on a plain beside the Santa Catarina River, this city offered General Pedro de Ampudia's army of 7,300 men a powerful defensive position. A strong fort called the Bishop's Palace stood high on Independence Hill to the west. In front of the city rose another fortress called the Citadel, while two forts, Teneria and Diablo, protected the eastern approaches. "In addition to these immense exterior defenses," observed Major Luther Giddings, "almost every street and square in the city was barricaded . . . and every house (being built in the old Mexican style, with thick walls and stone roofs) was a fortress."

Above: General Pedro de Ampudia
Right: General William Worth

In conference with his officers, Taylor decided to split his army. Brigadier General William Worth was to lead the main attack against Independence Hill. At the same time Lieutenant Colonel John Garland's division would threaten the eastern part of the city. Turning to Garland, Taylor ordered: "Colonel, lead the head of your columns off to the left, keeping out of reach of the enemy's shot, and if you think . . . you can take any of them little forts down there with the bay'net you better do it."

On September 21 the Americans charged Monterrey from both sides. Cannon at the Bishop's Palace boomed as Worth's troops encircled Independence Hill. Running recklessly forward through the narrow streets, Garland's soldiers met with a perfect storm of gunfire.

"We . . . had advanced but a short distance," declared Captain William S. Henry, "when we came suddenly upon an unknown battery, which opened its deadly fire upon us. From all its embrasures, from every house, from every yard, showers of balls were hurled upon us. . . ."

Garland's brave troops captured Fort Teneria, but his cost in dead and wounded amounted to 394 men.

On September 22, after a night of drenching rain, General Worth's soldiers scaled the peaks of Independence Hill and the walls of the Bishop's Palace. Musket flashes and clouds of smoke rolled steadily up the hillside. "Our men could be seen climbing up from rock to rock," noted Lieutenant French. "Through the rifts of smoke we saw our men leaping over the parapets, and the Mexicans retreating down the slope."

The Americans had captured both the eastern and western approaches to Monterrey. On the third day of battle the two halves of Taylor's army began a pincer movement, fighting house by house and street by street toward the center of the city. Captain Henry exclaimed that the "troops fought most gallantly, drawing the enemy before them . . . their rifles picking them off wherever a Mexican's body or head presented itself." Scrambling over barricades and even tunneling through walls, the Americans steadily advanced. Still the Mexicans savagely resisted, firing from doorways, windows, and roofs, sweeping the streets with gunfire, "as if bushels of hickory nuts were hurled at us," remembered Captain Henry. "Go it, my boys!" officers yelled, and the Americans kept rushing ahead.

Throughout the day Taylor stayed with his men, giving orders and encouragement. "General Taylor was in town with his staff, on foot, walking about, perfectly regardless of danger," noticed Captain Henry with surprise. "He was very imprudent in the exposure of his person. He crossed the street in which there was such a terrible fire in a walk, and by every chance should have been shot. I ran across with some of my men, and reminded him how much he was exposing himself, to which he replied, 'Take that ax and knock in that door.'"

Private Upton later declared, "Every house was a castle and filled with soldiers. The riflemen soon made them clear as fast as they could. They all retreated to the neighborhood of the plaza, or publick square. . . . We found a great many guns, etc. concealed in the houses. I saw Old Zack munching a piece of *pan* (gingerbread) and *pelonse* (sugar) which he found in a store."

At sunset Taylor's bloodied troops were only one square away from the central plaza. All seemed hopeless for the Mexicans now. On the morning of September 24, General Ampudia rode to Taylor's headquarters tent and offered to surrender.

His men tired, supplies running short, and desiring to win peace, Taylor agreed to generous terms. He accepted the surrender of Monterrey with all its public property, but allowed the Mexican army to march away to the south. In addition, he agreed not to pursue the enemy for eight weeks.

"These terms are liberal," he later remarked, "but not considered too much so by all reflecting men."

Above: General Taylor at Monterrey
Below: The storming of Independence Hill at Monterrey

The main plaza of Mexico City

On September 25 the Americans formally marched into the city. As a band blared "Yankee Doodle," many dusty soldiers sang along and cheered. The victory had cost the Americans 488 casualties and the Mexicans 367.

In Washington, President Polk greeted news of the surrender terms with anger. Polk, a Democrat, wanted the Mexican army crushed before his Whig political enemies could use the war as an election weapon against him. "I am now satisfied," the president complained, "that anybody would do better than Taylor. Taylor is no doubt brave and will fight, but is not fit for a higher command than that of a regiment. I have no prejudice against him, but think he has acted with great weakness and folly."

President Polk's criticisms hurt Taylor's feelings but not his popularity. Though his tactics were sometimes clumsy and he was often lucky, still Taylor won his battles and Americans loved him for it. Some Whig leaders even talked of running Taylor for president in 1848.

Major General Winfield Scott

Through the fall of 1846 Taylor's army strengthened its position in northern Mexico. Taylor suggested that the next military campaign be an inland march from coastal Vera Cruz to Mexico City. The War Department accepted this plan but, to reduce Old Rough and Ready's popularity and importance, President Polk placed Major General Winfield Scott in command of the operation. As army chief of staff, General Scott sent orders stripping nine thousand veteran troops from Taylor's army for his use.

Upon first reading these orders, Taylor became so furious that he absentmindedly spooned mustard instead of sugar into the coffee he was drinking. The president, he realized, intended to take him out of action. Hurt and outraged, still Taylor resolved to do his duty. "I will carry out in good faith . . . the views of the government," he vowed, "though I may be sacrificed in the effort."

In January 1847, General Taylor watched with pride and affection as his summoned troops departed for the seacoast. With the remains of his army, Taylor pushed eighty miles southwest from Monterrey to the town of Agua Nueva to hold a defensive position.

Soon rumors reached camp that General Antonio López de Santa Anna, the new Mexican commander-in-chief, was marching a vast army northward to destroy Taylor's weakened forces. "Should they offer us battle," Taylor insisted, "I shall indulge them be the consequences what they may." "Let them come," he told a visiting newspaperman, swearing they would "go back a good deal faster than they came!"

By February 19, American scouts reported the approach of a Mexican army of more than fifteen thousand men. On the advice of General John E. Wool, Taylor withdrew his troops several miles north to a ranch called Buena Vista. Here the ground offered the Americans an especially strong defensive position.

Lieutenant French described the area: "If the Hudson river, where it passes through the Catskill Mountains, were dry and wider, and its surface furrowed by deep ravines and water gullies crossing it, it would resemble the field of Buena Vista."

Through the morning of February 22, Taylor's 4,600 men collected supplies and fortified the mountain pass. "It will be a dreadful fight," predicted one soldier, William P. Rogers, "but we can not be whipped by a Mexican Army. . . . The whole [American] army has . . . confidence in General Taylor."

General
Antonio
López de
Santa Anna

Complete faith in Old Rough and Ready would surely be needed if these men were to beat the enemy army that began arriving in the afternoon. "The advance guard of the Mexicans," exclaimed Private Chamberlain, "consisted of a brigade of Lancers and a battery of Horse Artillery. They advanced in fine style, winding in and out of the ravines, with a fine brass band playing, until they had approached within a mile of our line. . . . Heavy masses of infantry and numerous batteries of guns now came in sight, marching in beautiful array, firm and steady as if on parade. On they came, until the whole country in our front was covered with their dense masses."

From these ranks some horsemen with a flag of truce galloped forward. They presented Taylor with a surrender demand from General Santa Anna.

"You are surrounded by twenty thousand men," it read, "and cannot . . . avoid suffering a rout, and being cut to pieces with your troops."

In answer to this personal threat, General Taylor exploded, "Tell Santa Anna to go to hell!"

Using more diplomatic language, Taylor's aide, Major W. W. Bliss, wrote a formal refusal of the Mexican demand, which the enemy horsemen carried back to their lines. During the daylight hours remaining, Mexican infantry pressed against the flanks of Taylor's line to test the Americans' strength.

Fearing an attack on his supply depot in Saltillo to the north, Taylor traveled there in the darkness with reinforcements. On February 23, 1847, action commenced at Buena Vista long before Taylor returned.

"The skirmish in the mountain opened lively," remembered Private Chamberlain. Soon General Santa Anna sent regiment after regiment into the smoking fray. Dozens of Americans fell in wounded agony. Although they fought ferociously, as the battle raged Taylor's outnumbered troops began to give ground.

It was then that Old Rough and Ready reached the field with his escort of dragoons and Mississippi riflemen. The hurried V formation of Colonel Jefferson Davis's red-shirted men foiled the flanking attack of Mexican lancers. With his arms calmly crossed, Taylor sat sideways on his white charger in sight of all his troops. One bullet ripped his coat sleeve. Another tore through the front of his coat, taking a button with it. Still Taylor remained unbothered, issuing orders and watching the fight.

General Taylor commanding his troops at Buena Vista

Inspired by their general's cool courage, the soldiers around him rallied. With the timely arrival of Bragg's artillery pieces, the remains of Santa Anna's forces retreated down the gorge.

The next morning Taylor expected another Mexican attack, but discovered the enemy was gone. Many brave officers and enlisted men lay bloody on the field. The Americans had suffered 673 casualties, while the Mexicans had lost about 1,800. Taylor generously commended the brave men who had held the mountain pass.

GRAND TRIUMPHAL QUICK STEP,

COMPOSED & DEDICATED TO

Gen. Zachary Taylor,

by

EDWARD L. WHITE,

BOSTON.

Published by OLIVER DITSON, 115 Washington St.

Entered according to act of Congress AD 1847 by O. Ditson in the Clerks Office of the district Court of Mass

Rafford & Co Lith.

25 cts nett

A musical composition honoring Taylor and his victories

Buena Vista proved to be Zachary Taylor's last battle. Through the summer and fall, General Scott conducted his successful invasion of central Mexico, which ended with the capture of Mexico City. During that time Taylor held his northern position, sending troops here and there to fight Mexican cavalry raiders.

Opposite page: Special music written for
Taylor's visit to New Orleans in 1847

GRAND TRIUMPHAL MARCH

Composed and respectfully dedicated

TO

MAJ. GEN. ZACH. TAYLOR

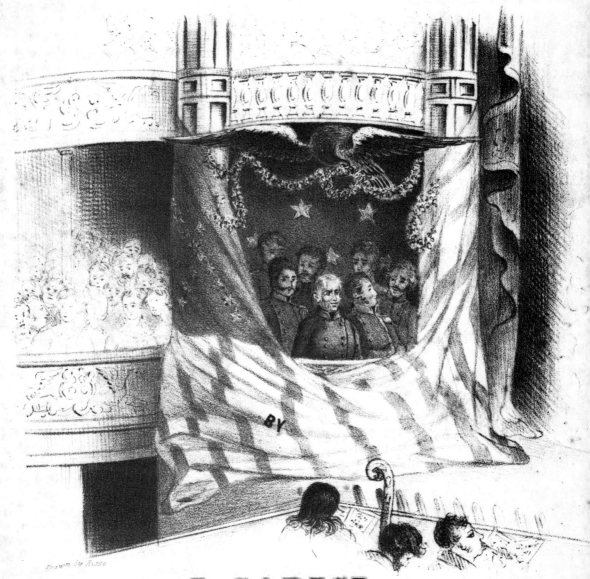

Drawn by Russo

BY

L. GABICI

Leader of the Orchestra of the Saint Charles Theatre

Performed on the occasion of the General's Visit to

that establishment, Dec.r 3, 1847.

GENERAL ZACHARIAH TAYLOR, (OLD ROUGH AND READY.)

A picture of Taylor, showing his unusual way of sitting on his horse

Chapter 7

The Reluctant Candidate

In the United States, Taylor's victory at Buena Vista threw Americans into a frenzy of celebration. For the fourth time in a row, Zachary Taylor had beaten a much larger Mexican army. Now more than ever, Whig politicians wished to run this plain, unassuming, homespun hero for president.

Months earlier, officers sitting casually in Taylor's headquarters tent mentioned their general as a possible candidate. In answer Taylor gruffly laughed, "Stop your nonsense and drink your whiskey." When an important Whig, Thurlow Weed, predicted Taylor would be elected president, Old Rough and Ready remarked that the idea "seems to me too visionary to require a serious answer. . . . [It] never entered my head, nor is it likely to enter the head of any sane person." He insisted that he was a soldier and not a politician. "I do not care a fig about the office," he proclaimed. He even openly admitted he had never voted in a presidential election. Years at frontier outposts kept him too busy for such things.

In time, however, the general changed his mind. Newspapers received in camp, as well as a constant flow of letters, all urged him to run. This attention flattered him and, stung by President Polk's unfriendly treatment, Taylor finally agreed to serve as president—"if the good people are imprudent enough to elect me."

With the Mexican War nearly over, Taylor requested a six-month leave of absence from the army. In November 1847, he sailed homeward for a well-deserved rest. Through the next months the old warrior relaxed with his family at Baton Rouge, while Americans still clamored for him to run for president. Finally, in April 1848, he officially offered himself as a possible Whig candidate.

Two months later, Whig delegates assembled in Philadelphia for their 1848 national convention. Many delegates proclaimed Zachary Taylor their favorite candidate for nomination. Other names considered were General Winfield Scott, Senator Henry Clay, and Senator Daniel Webster. Daniel Webster tried to dismiss Taylor as little more than "a swearing, whiskey-drinking, fighting frontier colonel." But Old Rough and Ready proved too popular for his rivals. On the fourth ballot Taylor obtained enough votes to win the nomination as Whig presidential candidate. As nominee for vice-president, the Whigs chose New Yorker Millard Fillmore.

Promptly the Whig convention sent Taylor official notice of his nomination and awaited his acceptance. The letter, however, arrived at Baton Rouge with postage due, and Taylor, always thrifty, refused to pay it. The general had been receiving a lot of collect mail from admirers,

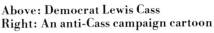

Above: Democrat Lewis Cass
Right: An anti-Cass campaign cartoon

and, tired of the expense, he finally ordered such letters returned unread. When the Whigs realized their mistake, they posted a second letter, prepaid.

Taylor received his important news with humility. "I feel duly grateful for the honor bestowed on me," he announced. "I cordially accept that nomination, but with the sincere distrust of my fitness to fulfill the duties of . . . office."

To oppose Taylor, the Democratic party nominated Lewis Cass. Cass was a distinguished veteran of the War of 1812 and longtime governor of the Michigan Territory. He had served as President Andrew Jackson's secretary of war and later as minister to France.

An 1848 cartoon depicting President Polk, Zachary Taylor, and Lewis Cass

Cass openly favored American expansion into the Oregon Territory and the lands won as a result of the Mexican War. He believed the settlers in these regions should have the right to decide whether they wanted slavery or not. Through the 1840s a growing number of northerners believed slavery to be cruel and immoral. Unhappy with the selection of Cass, antislavery Democrats soon formed a separate political party to represent their views. With the slogan "Free Soil, Free Speech, Free Labor, Free Men," the new Free Soil party put forth ex-president Martin Van Buren as its 1848 presidential candidate.

Abraham Lincoln as a young lawyer

While the Democrats and Free Soilers argued about slavery, Zachary Taylor remained in Baton Rouge and kept his opinions to himself. In Washington, where Whig congressmen formed a Taylor club called the Young Indians, one member, Congressman Abraham Lincoln, gave an amusing speech in the House of Representatives. In it Lincoln insisted that Taylor's uncommitted stance allowed the people to decide the issues for themselves. In the South, Whigs reminded voters that Taylor owned slaves himself and probably favored their position. In the North and the West, Whig supporters emphasized Taylor's military record and enormous personal popularity.

Through the summer and fall of 1848, "Taylor fever" swept the country. Rough and Ready clubs paraded in the streets, held barbecues, and gathered at rallies. Pictures of General Taylor and the slogan "Rough and Ready" appeared everywhere. One New Yorker, J. B. Mowers, noted, "It is on the butcher's stall, it is in the market places. It is on the fish stands, it is on cigar boxes and other divers places." Several printed campaign songs glorified Taylor's army career. One included the words

> Old Zach's at Monterray
> Bring out your Santa Anner.
> For every time we raise a gun
> Down goes a Mexicanner.

Campaign biographies described Taylor's life and contained amusing stories that revealed his hardy character. One such anecdote told of a refined young volunteer who went to complain about camp conditions during the Florida Seminole War. "General," the young man addressed his commander, "you'll excuse me, but since I've been here I've been doing all I could for you—have, indeed; but the fact is, the accommodations are very bad . . . mud sir! [I'm obliged] to lie down in it, actually; and the fact is, general, I'm a *gentleman's son*, and not used to it. . . . What am I to do?" "Why, really," said Taylor, "I don't know, unless you take my place." "Well, now, that's civil—'tis, indeed," said the young man. "Of course don't mean to *turn you out*, but a few hours' sleep—a cot or a bunk, or anything—would be so refreshing! Your place—where is it, general?" "O," said Taylor, "just drop down—*anywhere about here*—any place about camp will answer!"

Stunned at first, the young man then smiled and said, "Well, no wonder they call you 'Rough and Ready!' "

For several months Whigs, Democrats, and Free Soilers fiercely campaigned for their candidates. At last election day arrived on November 7, 1848. For the first time, according to a new act of Congress, voters nationwide went to the polls on the same day. There they cast ballots for electors who pledged in turn to vote for specific candidates. Eagerly Americans awaited the results of the close contest. The clicking keys of Samuel F. B. Morse's four-year-old invention, the electromagnetic telegraph, speeded the counting process and soon announced the outcome:

	Popular Vote	Electoral Vote
Zachary Taylor	1,360,101	163
Lewis Cass	1,220,544	127
Martin Van Buren	291,263	-

The Free Soilers failed to carry the electoral votes of a single state. Van Buren's party, however, had sapped enough strength from the Democrats to determine who would win. By a margin of 139,557 votes, Zachary Taylor had been elected twelfth president of the United States.

At the end of January 1849, Taylor resigned from the United States Army. The sixty-four-year-old general had served faithfully in uniform for forty years. Before leaving for Washington he briefly addressed the people of Baton Rouge. "Although I fear I am not qualified to discharge the great and important duties imposed upon me," he told his audience, "yet be assured, fellow citizens, I shall endeavor to fulfill them without regard to fear, favor, or affection for any one."

Z. TAYLOR. M. FILLMORE.

THE PEOPLE'S CHOICE FOR

PRESIDENT & VICE PRESIDENT

FROM 1849 TO 1853.

GRAND, NATIONAL, WHIG BANNER.
PRESS ONWARD.

Chapter 8

A Strong Leader for a
Growing Nation

Crowds of people cheered and waved at every stop during Zachary Taylor's journey to the capital. Thousands more massed at the Washington railroad depot when his train arrived. One young man, John Pegrum, remembered, "such hurrahing, and pushing and knocking down, I never saw before." The station remained so packed, an hour passed before Taylor could reach a waiting carriage. "I thought the mob would have torn the horses and carriage into a thousand pieces," marveled Pegrum, "some were on the wheels, some *under* them, some had hold of the traces and all were aiming to have a peep at the old Hero."

Because inauguration day fell on Sunday, March 4, 1849, Taylor waited until Monday to be sworn in. Some historians therefore argue that David Rice Atchison, president pro tempore of the Senate, served as United States president for that single day.

Opposite page: Campaign banner
for the 1848 Whig convention

Despite an icy wind and a light snow, on the morning of March 5 excited people stood shoulder to shoulder along Pennsylvania Avenue to view the inaugural procession. Behind a horseback escort of one hundred marshalls, Zachary Taylor and departing president James K. Polk wheeled toward the Capitol together in an open carriage. Jamming the Capitol grounds, a crowd of thirty thousand watched the swearing-in ceremony. At noon, Taylor stepped out onto a special platform constructed on the steps of the Capitol's east portico. In a low voice the general read his brief inaugural address. He then took the oath of office from Supreme Court Chief Justice Roger B. Taney. Swearing to preserve and protect the Constitution, Zachary Taylor became the nation's twelfth president.

Taylor spent his first days as president picking loyal Whigs to head the government's departments and serve as his cabinet. Hundreds of other job seekers stalked the White House hallways seeking interviews. The swarm proved so insistent that Secretary of State John M. Clayton finally remarked that if the president "does not *kick* a man down-stairs he goes away and declares he *promised him* an office."

Additional people visited the White House just for a chance to meet Old Rough and Ready. An Englishwoman, Lady Wortley, paid a social call and reported: "His manners are winningly frank, simple, and kind. . . . there is not the slightest roughness in his address. . . . He was so exceedingly good-natured as to talk a great deal to my little girl about roses and lilies, as if he had been quite a botanist all his life."

President Taylor sometimes greeted men more casually. On arriving in his office one visitor remembered, "I was at once ushered into the presence of General Taylor who sat at his desk. The presidential feet rested on another chair. . . . He wore a shirt that was formally white, but which then looked like the map of Mexico after the battle of Buena Vista. It was spotted and splattered with tobacco juice." As they chatted, Taylor spit tobacco juice toward a cuspidor on the floor several feet away and "with . . . unerring . . . aim . . . he never missed the cuspidor once."

Often sickly, Mrs. Taylor disliked Washington and kept herself secluded in an upstairs White House bedroom. Therefore, twenty-two-year-old daughter Betty Taylor Bliss (married to Colonel W. W. Bliss, now the president's personal secretary) performed the duties of White House hostess at official dinners. President Taylor, however, preferred those open White House receptions where he could mingle with the people. Mr. D. W. Mitchell described one such summer evening:

"The military or Marine Band is playing excellent music in the garden of the White House, everybody walking in and out and about without restriction; the President perhaps strolling over the lawn among the company, ready to shake hands with any one who chooses to introduce himself. . . . public men, clerks, and groups of various kinds, are promenading, while children are gamboling about. Labourers roughly dressed stand or lounge on the grass; there is no guard, no police; all behaving themselves properly."

Whale hunters took small rowboats out from the larger ship to hunt whales.

The United States in 1849 and 1850 was a huge, thriving nation whose citizens enjoyed limitless opportunities. European immigrants gladly took jobs in northern factories, while southern plantation owners provided cotton for New England's textile mills. Sweating work parties lay the rails for the country's growing railroad network. American flags fluttered on hundreds of ships carrying trade goods across the Atlantic, and hardy Yankee sea captains cruised the far reaches of the Pacific Ocean hunting whales for their valuable oil.

Above: The inauguration of President Zachary Taylor on March 4, 1849

Right: Supreme Court Chief Justice Roger B. Taney, who administered the oath of office to Zachary Taylor

Prospectors panning for gold during the California gold rush

The 1848 Treaty of Guadalupe Hidalgo had ended the Mexican War and had won the United States 500,000 square miles of land, including the California and New Mexico territories. During that year the discovery of gold on John Sutter's Sacramento Valley estate sparked the great California gold rush. In 1849, more than 80,000 easterners swarmed to California to seek their fortunes. These "Forty-Niners," and the thousands who followed after them, shoveled and panned for gold and quickly settled the California Territory.

Zachary Taylor's administration helped guide the country through this period of enormous growth and progress. In Washington the new Department of the Interior managed the nation's Indian affairs, public lands, patent office, and census bureau. On an international level, the State Department arranged the Clayton-Bulwer Treaty between the United States and Great Britain in April 1850. The treaty was designed to insure peace in the region of Nicaragua and Costa Rica.

By far the greatest crisis facing Taylor's presidency was the issue of slavery. The southern slave states and northern free states remained violently divided on the question. Southern congressmen urged that slavery be extended into the California and New Mexico territories and fully expected President Taylor to support them.

Surprisingly, Taylor soon proved himself "a Southern man with Northern principles." In an August 1849 speech the president told a Mercer, Pennsylvania, audience, "The people of the North need have no apprehension of the further extension of slavery." He suggested California and New Mexico apply for statehood. Allowed to write their own state constitutions, they would most probably join the nation as free states.

This proposal enraged southerners who felt threatened by a possible imbalance between slave states and free states in the Senate. At the Capitol, congressional debate rose to such a fevered pitch that fistfights broke out from time to time, and some men carried guns for protection.

One day three southern congressmen met with Taylor and warned that their states might quit the Union altogether. Responding angrily, Taylor told them that "if it becomes necessary, in executing the laws, he would take command of the army himself, and that if they were taken in rebellion against the Union, he would hang them with less reluctance than he had hung deserters and spies in Mexico!" Later Senator Hannibal Hamlin of Maine entered the president's office and found the old man "rushing around the room like a caged lion." "Did you see those damned traitors," Taylor declared, shaking his fist.

While raging southerners and northerners threatened to tear the United States in two, Zachary Taylor at least remained a solid American. "We must . . . preserve the Union at all hazards," he insisted to his countrymen. "Upon its preservation must depend our own happiness and that of countless generations to come. Whatever dangers may threaten it, I stand by it."

In the Senate, the nation's greatest statesmen, John C. Calhoun of South Carolina, Daniel Webster of Massachusetts, and Henry Clay of Kentucky, searched for measures that would keep the North and South together. Stubbornly, however, Old Rough and Ready refused to consider any compromises. He was sure he could preserve the Union with armed force if necessary.

Historians guess that only Taylor's unexpected death enabled Henry Clay's famous 1850 compromise bills to pass into law. These bills allowed California to enter the United States as a free state, but also favored the South by extending interstate slave trade and requiring the capture and return of runaway slaves. "Clay's Compromise" kept the North and South at peace for another ten years. However, only the bloody American Civil War (1861-1865) would solve the problem of slavery once and for all.

As the 1850 slavery debate continued in Congress, sixty-five-year-old President Taylor took time to attend Fourth of July celebrations at the unfinished Washington Monument. Standing bareheaded under a blistering sun, Taylor watched workmen lay the monument's cornerstone. Bands filled the air with music and distinguished guests gave patriotic speeches.

Millard Fillmore

After the long, hot ceremony, Taylor gladly quenched his thirst with several glasses of ice water. Back at the White House, he further refreshed himself by eating handfuls of cherries and quarts of iced milk. That evening he suddenly fell ill with severe stomach cramps.

During the next five days, Taylor's condition steadily worsened as symptoms of cholera and typhoid fever set in. Tearful relatives, friends, and cabinet members gathered at his bedside on the evening of July 9, 1850. "I am about to die," he murmured. "I expect the summons very soon. I have endeavored to discharge all my official duties faithfully. I regret nothing, but am sorry that I am about to leave my friends."

Those were his final words. At 10:30 P.M. Zachary Taylor died, after serving only sixteen months as president. The next day Vice-President Millard Fillmore took the oath of office as thirteenth U.S. president.

The death of Zachary Taylor

In Washington, servants draped the White House in black and city cannon fired funeral salutes, as people learned the news of Taylor's death. On July 13 grieving thousands lined the route that carried Taylor's coffin to its temporary grave at the Congressional Burial Ground. In the solemn funeral procession, Taylor's faithful horse, Old Whitey, was walked close behind the hearse. Later Taylor's remains were reburied on his plantation beside Beargrass Creek near Louisville, Kentucky.

Across the country Americans mourned the loss of the hero of Buena Vista. The beloved old army officer had left

Taylor's funeral pageant in New York, July 30, 1850

his mark on the nation and its history. At the Capitol, congressmen respectfully gave speeches in tribute to his memory. Perhaps former rival Daniel Webster best summed up Taylor's qualities, stating that he left "on the minds of the country a strong impression, first of his absolute honesty and integrity of character; next, of his sound, practical good sense; and lastly, of the mildness, kindness, and friendliness of his temper towards all of his countrymen."

As Americans pressed forward to fulfill their destiny, time and time again they would remember the example set by the fearless general nicknamed Old Rough and Ready.

Chronology of American History

(Shaded area covers events in Zachary Taylor's lifetime.)

About A.D. 982 — Eric the Red, born in Norway, reaches Greenland in one of the first European voyages to North America.

About 985 — Eric the Red brings settlers from Iceland to Greenland.

About 1000 — Leif Ericson (Eric the Red's son) leads what is thought to be the first European expedition to mainland North America; Leif probably lands in Canada.

1492 — Christopher Columbus, seeking a sea route from Spain to the Far East, discovers the New World.

1497 — John Cabot reaches Canada in the first English voyage to North America.

1513 — Ponce de Léon explores Florida in search of the fabled Fountain of Youth.

1519-1521 — Hernando Cortés of Spain conquers Mexico.

1534 — French explorers led by Jacques Cartier enter the Gulf of St. Lawrence in Canada.

1540 — Spanish explorer Francisco Coronado begins exploring the American Southwest, seeking the riches of the mythical Seven Cities of Cibola.

1565 — St. Augustine, Florida, the first permanent European town in what is now the United States, is founded by the Spanish.

1607 — Jamestown, Virginia, is founded, the first permanent English town in the present-day U.S.

1608 — Frenchman Samuel de Champlain founds the village of Quebec, Canada.

1609 — Henry Hudson explores the eastern coast of present-day U.S. for the Netherlands; the Dutch then claim parts of New York, New Jersey, Delaware, and Connecticut and name the area New Netherland.

1619 — The English colonies' first shipment of black slaves arrives in Jamestown.

1620 — English Pilgrims found Massachusetts' first permanent town at Plymouth.

1621 — Massachusetts Pilgrims and Indians hold the famous first Thanksgiving feast in colonial America.

1623 — Colonization of New Hampshire is begun by the English.

1624 — Colonization of present-day New York State is begun by the Dutch at Fort Orange (Albany).

1625 — The Dutch start building New Amsterdam (now New York City).

1630 — The town of Boston, Massachusetts, is founded by the English Puritans.

1633 — Colonization of Connecticut is begun by the English.

1634 — Colonization of Maryland is begun by the English.

1636 — Harvard, the colonies' first college, is founded in Massachusetts. Rhode Island colonization begins when Englishman Roger Williams founds Providence.

1638 — Delaware colonization begins when Swedish people build Fort Christina at present-day Wilmington.

1640 — Stephen Daye of Cambridge, Massachusetts prints *The Bay Psalm Book*, the first English-language book published in what is now the U.S.

1643 — Swedish settlers begin colonizing Pennsylvania.

About 1650 — North Carolina is colonized by Virginia settlers.

1660 — New Jersey colonization is begun by the Dutch at present-day Jersey City.

1670 — South Carolina colonization is begun by the English near Charleston.

1673 — Jacques Marquette and Louis Jolliet explore the upper Mississippi River for France.

1682—Philadelphia, Pennsylvania, is settled. La Salle explores Mississippi River all the way to its mouth in Louisiana and claims the whole Mississippi Valley for France.

1693—College of William and Mary is founded in Williamsburg, Virginia.

1700—Colonial population is about 250,000.

1703—Benjamin Franklin is born in Boston.

1732—George Washington, first president of the U.S., is born in Westmoreland County, Virginia.

1733—James Oglethorpe founds Savannah, Georgia; Georgia is established as the thirteenth colony.

1735—John Adams, second president of the U.S., is born in Braintree, Massachusetts.

1737—William Byrd founds Richmond, Virginia.

1738—British troops are sent to Georgia over border dispute with Spain.

1739—Black insurrection takes place in South Carolina.

1740—English Parliament passes act allowing naturalization of immigrants to American colonies after seven-year residence.

1743—Thomas Jefferson, third president of the U.S., is born in Albemarle County, Virginia. Benjamin Franklin retires at age thirty-seven to devote himself to scientific inquiries and public service.

1744—King George's War begins; France joins war effort against England.

1745—During King George's War, France raids settlements in Maine and New York.

1747—Classes begin at Princeton College in New Jersey.

1748—The Treaty of Aix-la-Chapelle concludes King George's War.

1749—Parliament legally recognizes slavery in colonies and the inauguration of the plantation system in the South. George Washington becomes the surveyor for Culpepper County in Virginia.

1750—Thomas Walker passes through and names Cumberland Gap on his way toward Kentucky region. Colonial population is about 1,200,000.

1751—James Madison, fourth president of the U.S., is born in Port Conway, Virginia. English Parliament passes Currency Act, banning New England colonies from issuing paper money. George Washington travels to Barbados.

1752—Pennsylvania Hospital, the first general hospital in the colonies, is founded in Philadelphia. Benjamin Franklin uses a kite in a thunderstorm to demonstrate that lightning is a form of electricity.

1753—George Washington delivers command from Virginia Lieutenant Governor Dinwiddie that the French withdraw from the Ohio River Valley; French disregard the demand. Colonial population is about 1,328,000.

1754—French and Indian War begins (extends to Europe as the Seven Years' War). Washington surrenders at Fort Necessity.

1755—French and Indians ambush General Braddock. Washington becomes commander of Virginia troops.

1756—England declares war on France.

1758—James Monroe, fifth president of the U.S., is born in Westmoreland County, Virginia.

1759—Cherokee Indian war begins in southern colonies; hostilities extend to 1761. George Washington marries Martha Dandridge Custis.

1760—George III becomes king of England. Colonial population is about 1,600,000.

1762—England declares war on Spain.

1763—Treaty of Paris concludes the French and Indian War and the Seven Years' War. England gains Canada and most other French lands east of the Mississippi River.

1764—British pass the Sugar Act to gain tax money from the colonists. The issue of taxation without representation is first introduced in Boston. John Adams marries Abigail Smith.

1765—Stamp Act goes into effect in the colonies. Business virtually stops as almost all colonists refuse to use the stamps.

1766—British repeal the Stamp Act.

1767—John Quincy Adams, sixth president of the U.S. and son of second president John Adams, is born in Braintree, Massachusetts. Andrew Jackson, seventh president of the U.S., is born in Waxhaw settlement, South Carolina.

1769—Daniel Boone sights the Kentucky Territory.

1770—In the Boston Massacre, British soldiers kill five colonists and injure six. Townshend Acts are repealed, thus eliminating all duties on imports to the colonies except tea.

1771—Benjamin Franklin begins his autobiography, a work that he will never complete. The North Carolina assembly passes the "Bloody Act," which makes rioters guilty of treason.

1772—Samuel Adams rouses colonists to consider British threats to self-government. Thomas Jefferson marries Martha Wayles Skelton.

1773—English Parliament passes the Tea Act. Colonists dressed as Mohawk Indians board British tea ships and toss 342 casks of tea into the water in what becomes known as the Boston Tea Party. William Henry Harrison is born in Charles City County, Virginia.

1774—British close the port of Boston to punish the city for the Boston Tea Party. First Continental Congress convenes in Philadelphia.

1775—American Revolution begins with battles of Lexington and Concord, Massachusetts. Second Continental Congress opens in Philadelphia. George Washington becomes commander-in-chief of the Continental army.

1776—Declaration of Independence is adopted on July 4.

1777—Congress adopts the American flag with thirteen stars and thirteen stripes. John Adams is sent to France to negotiate peace treaty.

1778—France declares war against Great Britain and becomes U.S. ally.

1779—British surrender to Americans at Vincennes. Thomas Jefferson is elected governor of Virginia. James Madison is elected to the Continental Congress.

1780—Benedict Arnold, first American traitor, defects to the British.

1781—Articles of Confederation go into effect. Cornwallis surrenders to George Washington at Yorktown, ending the American Revolution.

1782—American commissioners, including John Adams, sign peace treaty with British in Paris. Thomas Jefferson's wife, Martha, dies. Martin Van Buren is born in Kinderhook, New York.

1784—Zachary Taylor is born near Barboursville, Virginia.

1785—Congress adopts the dollar as the unit of currency. John Adams is made minister to Great Britain. Thomas Jefferson is appointed minister to France.

1786—Shays' Rebellion begins in Massachusetts.

1787—Constitutional Convention assembles in Philadelphia, with George Washington presiding; U.S. Constitution is adopted. Delaware, New Jersey, and Pennsylvania become states.

1788—Virginia, South Carolina, New York, Connecticut, New Hampshire, Maryland, and Massachusetts become states. U.S. Constitution is ratified. New York City is declared U.S. capital.

1789—Presidential electors elect George Washington and John Adams as first president and vice-president. Thomas Jefferson is appointed secretary of state. North Carolina becomes a state. French Revolution begins.

1790—Supreme Court meets for the first time. Rhode Island becomes a state. First national census in the U.S. counts 3,929,214 persons. John Tyler is born in Charles City County, Virginia.

1791—Vermont enters the Union. U.S. Bill of Rights, the first ten amendments to the Constitution, goes into effect. District of Columbia is established.

1792—Thomas Paine publishes *The Rights of Man*. Kentucky becomes a state. Two political parties are formed in the U.S., Federalist and Republican. Washington is elected to a second term, with Adams as vice-president.

1793—War between France and Britain begins; U.S. declares neutrality. Eli Whitney invents the cotton gin; cotton production and slave labor increase in the South.

1794—Eleventh Amendment to the Constitution is passed, limiting federal courts' power. "Whiskey Rebellion" in Pennsylvania protests federal whiskey tax. James Madison marries Dolley Payne Todd.

1795—George Washington signs the Jay Treaty with Great Britain. Treaty of San Lorenzo, between U.S. and Spain, settles Florida boundary and gives U.S. right to navigate the Mississippi. James Polk is born near Pineville, North Carolina.

1796—Tennessee enters the Union. Washington gives his Farewell Address, refusing a third presidential term. John Adams is elected president and Thomas Jefferson vice-president.

1797—Adams recommends defense measures against possible war with France. Napoleon Bonaparte and his army march against Austrians in Italy. U.S. population is about 4,900,000.

1798—Washington is named commander-in-chief of the U.S. army. Department of the Navy is created. Alien and Sedition Acts are passed. Napoleon's troops invade Egypt and Switzerland.

1799—George Washington dies at Mount Vernon. James Monroe is elected governor of Virginia. French Revolution ends. Napoleon becomes ruler of France.

1800—Thomas Jefferson and Aaron Burr tie for president. U.S. capital is moved from Philadelphia to Washington, D.C. The White House is built as presidents' home. Spain returns Louisiana to France. Millard Fillmore is born in Locke, New York.

1801—After thirty-six ballots, House of Representatives elects Thomas Jefferson president, making Burr vice-president. James Madison is named secretary of state.

1802—Congress abolishes excise taxes. U.S. Military Academy is founded at West Point, New York.

1803—Ohio enters the Union. Louisiana Purchase treaty is signed with France, greatly expanding U.S. territory.

1804—Twelfth Amendment to the Constitution rules that president and vice-president be elected separately. Alexander Hamilton is killed by Vice-President Aaron Burr in a duel. Orleans Territory is established. Napoleon crowns himself emperor of France.

1805—Thomas Jefferson begins his second term as president. Lewis and Clark expedition reaches the Pacific Ocean.

1806—Coinage of silver dollars is stopped; resumes in 1836.

1807—Aaron Burr is acquitted in treason trial. Embargo Act closes U.S. ports to trade.

1808—James Madison is elected president. Congress outlaws importing slaves from Africa.

1810—U.S. population is 7,240,000.

1811—William Henry Harrison defeats Indians at Tippecanoe. Monroe is named secretary of state.

1812—Louisiana becomes a state. U.S. declares war on Britain (War of 1812). James Madison is reelected president. Napoleon invades Russia.

1813—British forces take Fort Niagara and Buffalo, New York.

1814—Francis Scott Key writes "The Star-Spangled Banner." British troops burn much of Washington, D.C., including the White House. Treaty of Ghent ends War of 1812. James Monroe becomes secretary of war.

1815—Napoleon meets his final defeat at Battle of Waterloo.

1816—James Monroe is elected president. Indiana becomes a state.

1817—Mississippi becomes a state. Construction on Erie Canal begins.

1821—Missouri enters the Union as a slave state. Santa Fe Trail opens the American Southwest. Mexico declares independence from Spain. Napoleon Bonaparte dies.

1822—U.S. recognizes Mexico and Colombia. Liberia in Africa is founded as a home for freed slaves. Ulysses S. Grant is born in Point Pleasant, Ohio. Rutherford B. Hayes is born in Delaware, Ohio.

1823—Monroe Doctrine closes North and South America to European colonizing or invasion.

1824—House of Representatives elects John Quincy Adams president when none of the four candidates wins a majority in national election. Mexico becomes a republic.

1825—Erie Canal is opened. U.S. population is 11,300,000.

1826—Thomas Jefferson and John Adams both die on July 4, the fiftieth anniversary of the Declaration of Independence.

1828—Andrew Jackson is elected president. Tariff of Abominations is passed, cutting imports.

1829—James Madison attends Virginia's constitutional convention. Slavery is abolished in Mexico. Chester A. Arthur is born in Fairfield, Vermont.

1830—Indian Removal Act to resettle Indians west of the Mississippi is approved.

1831—James Monroe dies in New York City. James A. Garfield is born in Orange, Ohio. Cyrus McCormick develops his reaper.

1832—Andrew Jackson, nominated by the new Democratic Party, is reelected president.

1833—Britain abolishes slavery in its colonies. Benjamin Harrison is born in North Bend, Ohio.

1835—Federal government becomes debt-free for the first time.

1836—Martin Van Buren becomes president. Texas wins independence from Mexico. Arkansas joins the Union. James Madison dies at Montpelier, Virginia.

1837—Michigan enters the Union. U.S. population is 15,900,000. Grover Cleveland is born in Caldwell, New Jersey.

1840—William Henry Harrison is elected president.

1841—President Harrison dies in Washington, D.C., one month after inauguration. Vice-President John Tyler succeeds him.

1843—William McKinley is born in Niles, Ohio.

1844—James Knox Polk is elected president. Samuel Morse sends first telegraphic message.

1845—Texas and Florida become states. Potato famine in Ireland causes massive emigration from Ireland to U.S. Andrew Jackson dies near Nashville, Tennessee.

1846—Iowa enters the Union. War with Mexico begins.

1847—U.S. captures Mexico City.

1848—John Quincy Adams dies in Washington, D.C. Zachary Taylor becomes president. Treaty of Guadalupe Hidalgo ends Mexico-U.S. war. Wisconsin becomes a state.

1849—James Polk dies in Nashville, Tennessee.

1850—President Taylor dies in Washington, D.C.; Vice-President Millard Fillmore succeeds him. California enters the Union, breaking tie between slave and free states.

1852—Franklin Pierce is elected president.

1853—Gadsden Purchase transfers Mexican territory to U.S.

1854—"War for Bleeding Kansas" is fought between slave and free states.

1855—Czar Nicholas I of Russia dies, succeeded by Alexander II.

1856—James Buchanan is elected president. In Massacre of Potawatomi Creek, Kansas-slavers are murdered by free-staters. Woodrow Wilson is born in Staunton, Virginia.

1857—William Howard Taft is born in Cincinnati, Ohio.

1858—Minnesota enters the Union. Theodore Roosevelt is born in New York City.

1859—Oregon becomes a state.

1860 — Abraham Lincoln is elected president; South Carolina secedes from the Union in protest.

1861 — Arkansas, Tennessee, North Carolina, and Virginia secede. Kansas enters the Union as a free state. Civil War begins.

1862 — Union forces capture Fort Henry, Roanoke Island, Fort Donelson, Jacksonville, and New Orleans; Union armies are defeated at the battles of Bull Run and Fredericksburg. Martin Van Buren dies in Kinderhook, New York. John Tyler dies near Charles City, Virginia.

1863 — Lincoln issues Emancipation Proclamation: all slaves held in rebelling territories are declared free. West Virginia becomes a state.

1864 — Abraham Lincoln is reelected. Nevada becomes a state.

1865 — Lincoln is assassinated in Washington, D.C., and succeeded by Andrew Johnson. U.S. Civil War ends on May 26. Thirteenth Amendment abolishes slavery. Warren G. Harding is born in Blooming Grove, Ohio.

1867 — Nebraska becomes a state. U.S. buys Alaska from Russia for $7,200,000. Reconstruction Acts are passed.

1868 — President Johnson is impeached for violating Tenure of Office Act, but is acquitted by Senate. Ulysses S. Grant is elected president. Fourteenth Amendment prohibits voting discrimination. James Buchanan dies in Lancaster, Pennsylvania.

1869 — Franklin Pierce dies in Concord, New Hampshire.

1870 — Fifteenth Amendment gives blacks the right to vote.

1872 — Grant is reelected over Horace Greeley. General Amnesty Act pardons ex-Confederates. Calvin Coolidge is born in Plymouth Notch, Vermont.

1874 — Millard Fillmore dies in Buffalo, New York. Herbert Hoover is born in West Branch, Iowa.

1875 — Andrew Johnson dies in Carter's Station, Tennessee.

1876 — Colorado enters the Union. "Custer's last stand": he and his men are massacred by Sioux Indians at Little Big Horn, Montana.

1877 — Rutherford B. Hayes is elected president as all disputed votes are awarded to him.

1880 — James A. Garfield is elected president.

1881 — President Garfield is assassinated and dies in Elberon, New Jersey. Vice-President Chester A. Arthur succeeds him.

1882 — U.S. bans Chinese immigration. Franklin D. Roosevelt is born in Hyde Park, New York.

1884 — Grover Cleveland is elected president. Harry S. Truman is born in Lamar, Missouri.

1885 — Ulysses S. Grant dies in Mount McGregor, New York.

1886 — Statue of Liberty is dedicated. Chester A. Arthur dies in New York City.

1888 — Benjamin Harrison is elected president.

1889 — North Dakota, South Dakota, Washington, and Montana become states.

1890 — Dwight D. Eisenhower is born in Denison, Texas. Idaho and Wyoming become states.

1892 — Grover Cleveland is elected president.

1893 — Rutherford B. Hayes dies in Fremont, Ohio.

1896 — William McKinley is elected president. Utah becomes a state.

1898 — U.S. declares war on Spain over Cuba.

1900 — McKinley is reelected. Boxer Rebellion against foreigners in China begins.

1901 — McKinley is assassinated by anarchist Leon Czolgosz in Buffalo, New York; Theodore Roosevelt becomes president. Benjamin Harrison dies in Indianapolis, Indiana.

1902 — U.S. acquires perpetual control over Panama Canal.

1903 — Alaskan frontier is settled.

1904 — Russian-Japanese War breaks out. Theodore Roosevelt wins presidential election.

1905—Treaty of Portsmouth signed, ending Russian-Japanese War.

1906—U.S. troops occupy Cuba.

1907—President Roosevelt bars all Japanese immigration. Oklahoma enters the Union.

1908—William Howard Taft becomes president. Grover Cleveland dies in Princeton, New Jersey. Lyndon B. Johnson is born near Stonewall, Texas.

1909—NAACP is founded under W.E.B. DuBois

1910—China abolishes slavery.

1911—Chinese Revolution begins. Ronald Reagan is born in Tampico, Illinois.

1912—Woodrow Wilson is elected president. Arizona and New Mexico become states.

1913—Federal income tax is introduced in U.S. through the Sixteenth Amendment. Richard Nixon is born in Yorba Linda, California. Gerald Ford is born in Omaha, Nebraska.

1914—World War I begins.

1915—British liner *Lusitania* is sunk by German submarine.

1916—Wilson is reelected president.

1917—U.S. breaks diplomatic relations with Germany. Czar Nicholas of Russia abdicates as revolution begins. U.S. declares war on Austria-Hungary. John F. Kennedy is born in Brookline, Massachusetts.

1918—Wilson proclaims "Fourteen Points" as war aims. On November 11, armistice is signed between Allies and Germany.

1919—Eighteenth Amendment prohibits sale and manufacture of intoxicating liquors. Wilson presides over first League of Nations; wins Nobel Peace Prize. Theodore Roosevelt dies in Oyster Bay, New York.

1920—Nineteenth Amendment (women's suffrage) is passed. Warren Harding is elected president.

1921—Adolf Hitler's stormtroopers begin to terrorize political opponents.

1922—Irish Free State is established. Soviet states form USSR. Benito Mussolini forms Fascist government in Italy.

1923—President Harding dies in San Francisco, California; he is succeeded by Vice-President Calvin Coolidge.

1924—Coolidge is elected president. Woodrow Wilson dies in Washington, D.C. James Carter is born in Plains, Georgia. George Bush is born in Milton, Massachusetts.

1925—Hitler reorganizes Nazi Party and publishes first volume of *Mein Kampf.*

1926—Fascist youth organizations founded in Germany and Italy. Republic of Lebanon proclaimed.

1927—Stalin becomes Soviet dictator. Economic conference in Geneva attended by fifty-two nations.

1928—Herbert Hoover is elected president. U.S. and many other nations sign Kellogg-Briand pacts to outlaw war.

1929—Stock prices in New York crash on "Black Thursday"; the Great Depression begins.

1930—Bank of U.S. and its many branches close (most significant bank failure of the year). William Howard Taft dies in Washington, D.C.

1931—Emigration from U.S. exceeds immigration for first time as Depression deepens.

1932—Franklin D. Roosevelt wins presidential election in a Democratic landslide.

1933—First concentration camps are erected in Germany. U.S. recognizes USSR and resumes trade. Twenty-First Amendment repeals prohibition. Calvin Coolidge dies in Northampton, Massachusetts.

1934—Severe dust storms hit Plains states. President Roosevelt passes U.S. Social Security Act.

1936—Roosevelt is reelected. Spanish Civil War begins. Hitler and Mussolini form Rome-Berlin Axis.

1937—Roosevelt signs Neutrality Act.

1938—Roosevelt sends appeal to Hitler and Mussolini to settle European problems amicably.

1939—Germany takes over Czechoslovakia and invades Poland, starting World War II.

1940—Roosevelt is reelected for a third term.

1941—Japan bombs Pearl Harbor, U.S. declares war on Japan. Germany and Italy declare war on U.S.; U.S. then declares war on them.

1942—Allies agree not to make separate peace treaties with the enemies. U.S. government transfers more than 100,000 Nisei (Japanese-Americans) from west coast to inland concentration camps.

1943—Allied bombings of Germany begin.

1944—Roosevelt is reelected for a fourth term. Allied forces invade Normandy on D-Day.

1945—President Franklin D. Roosevelt dies in Warm Springs, Georgia; Vice-President Harry S. Truman succeeds him. Mussolini is killed; Hitler commits suicide. Germany surrenders. U.S. drops atomic bomb on Hiroshima; Japan surrenders: end of World War II.

1946—U.N. General Assembly holds its first session in London. Peace conference of twenty-one nations is held in Paris.

1947—Peace treaties are signed in Paris. "Cold War" is in full swing.

1948—U.S. passes Marshall Plan Act, providing $17 billion in aid for Europe. U.S. recognizes new nation of Israel. India and Pakistan become free of British rule. Truman is elected president.

1949—Republic of Eire is proclaimed in Dublin. Russia blocks land route access from Western Germany to Berlin; airlift begins. U.S., France, and Britain agree to merge their zones of occupation in West Germany. Apartheid program begins in South Africa.

1950—Riots in Johannesburg, South Africa, against apartheid. North Korea invades South Korea. U.N. forces land in South Korea and recapture Seoul.

1951—Twenty-Second Amendment limits president to two terms.

1952—Dwight D. Eisenhower resigns as supreme commander in Europe and is elected president.

1953—Stalin dies; struggle for power in Russia follows. Rosenbergs are executed for espionage.

1954—U.S. and Japan sign mutual defense agreement.

1955—Blacks in Montgomery, Alabama, boycott segregated bus lines.

1956—Eisenhower is reelected president. Soviet troops march into Hungary.

1957—U.S. agrees to withdraw ground forces from Japan. Russia launches first satellite, *Sputnik*.

1958—European Common Market comes into being. Fidel Castro begins war against Batista government in Cuba.

1959—Alaska becomes the forty-ninth state. Hawaii becomes fiftieth state. Castro becomes premier of Cuba. De Gaulle is proclaimed president of the Fifth Republic of France.

1960—Historic debates between Senator John F. Kennedy and Vice-President Richard Nixon are televised. Kennedy is elected president. Brezhnev becomes president of USSR.

1961—Berlin Wall is constructed. Kennedy and Khrushchev confer in Vienna. In Bay of Pigs incident, Cubans trained by CIA attempt to overthrow Castro.

1962—U.S. military council is established in South Vietnam.

1963—Riots and beatings by police and whites mark civil rights demonstrations in Birmingham, Alabama; 30,000 troops are called out, Martin Luther King, Jr., is arrested. Freedom marchers descend on Washington, D.C., to demonstrate. President Kennedy is assassinated in Dallas, Texas; Vice-President Lyndon B. Johnson is sworn in as president.

1964—U.S. aircraft bomb North Vietnam. Johnson is elected president. Herbert Hoover dies in New York City.

1965—U.S. combat troops arrive in South Vietnam.

1966—Thousands protest U.S. policy in Vietnam. National Guard quells race riots in Chicago.

1967—Six-Day War between Israel and Arab nations.

1968—Martin Luther King, Jr., is assassinated in Memphis, Tennessee. Senator Robert Kennedy is assassinated in Los Angeles. Riots and police brutality take place at Democratic National Convention in Chicago. Richard Nixon is elected president. Czechoslovakia is invaded by Soviet troops.

1969—Dwight D. Eisenhower dies in Washington, D.C. Hundreds of thousands of people in several U.S. cities demonstrate against Vietnam War.

1970—Four Vietnam War protesters are killed by National Guardsmen at Kent State University in Ohio.

1971—Twenty-Sixth Amendment allows eighteen-year-olds to vote.

1972—Nixon visits Communist China; is reelected president in near-record landslide. Watergate affair begins when five men are arrested in the Watergate hotel complex in Washington, D.C. Nixon announces resignations of aides Haldeman, Ehrlichman, and Dean and Attorney General Kleindienst as a result of Watergate-related charges. Harry S. Truman dies in Kansas City, Missouri.

1973—Vice-President Spiro Agnew resigns; Gerald Ford is named vice-president. Vietnam peace treaty is formally approved after nineteen months of negotiations. Lyndon B. Johnson dies in San Antonio, Texas.

1974—As a result of Watergate cover-up, impeachment is considered; Nixon resigns and Ford becomes president. Ford pardons Nixon and grants limited amnesty to Vietnam War draft evaders and military deserters.

1975—U.S. civilians are evacuated from Saigon, South Vietnam, as Communist forces complete takeover of South Vietnam.

1976—U.S. celebrates its Bicentennial. James Earl Carter becomes president.

1977—Carter pardons most Vietnam draft evaders, numbering some 10,000.

1980—Ronald Reagan is elected president.

1981—President Reagan is shot in the chest in assassination attempt. Sandra Day O'Connor is appointed first woman justice of the Supreme Court.

1983—U.S. troops invade island of Grenada.

1984—Reagan is reelected president. Democratic candidate Walter Mondale's running mate, Geraldine Ferraro, is the first woman selected for vice-president by a major U.S. political party.

1985—Soviet Communist Party secretary Konstantin Chernenko dies; Mikhail Gorbachev succeeds him. U.S. and Soviet officials discuss arms control in Geneva. Reagan and Gorbachev hold summit conference in Geneva. Racial tensions accelerate in South Africa.

1986—Space shuttle *Challenger* explodes shortly after takeoff; crew of seven dies. U.S. bombs bases in Libya. Corazon Aquino defeats Ferdinand Marcos in Philippine presidential election.

1987—Iraqi missile rips the U.S. frigate *Stark* in the Persian Gulf, killing thirty-seven American sailors. Congress holds hearings to investigate sale of U.S. arms to Iran to finance Nicaraguan *contra* movement.

1988—President Reagan and Soviet leader Gorbachev sign INF treaty, eliminating intermediate nuclear forces. Severe drought sweeps the United States. George Bush is elected president.

1989—East Germany opens Berlin Wall, allowing citizens free exit. Communists lose control of governments in Poland, Romania, and Czechoslovakia. Chinese troops massacre over 1,000 pro-democracy student demonstrators in Beijing's Tiananmen Square.

1990—Iraq annexes Kuwait, provoking the threat of war. East and West Germany are reunited. The Cold War between the United States and the Soviet Union comes to a close. Several Soviet republics make moves toward independence.

1991—Backed by a coalition of members of the United Nations, U.S. troops drive Iraqis from Kuwait. Latvia, Lithuania, and Estonia withdraw from the USSR. The Soviet Union dissolves as its republics secede to form a Commonwealth of Independent States.

1992—U.N. forces fail to stop fighting in territories of former Yugoslavia. More than fifty people are killed and more than six hundred buildings burned in rioting in Los Angeles. U.S. unemployment reaches eight-year high. Hurricane Andrew devastates southern Florida and parts of Louisiana. International relief supplies and troops are sent to combat famine and violence in Somalia.

1993—U.S.-led forces use airplanes and missiles to attack military targets in Iraq. William Jefferson Clinton becomes the forty-second U.S. president.

1994—Richard M. Nixon dies in New York City.

Index

Page numbers in boldface type indicate illustrations.

About the Author

Zachary Kent grew up in Little Falls, New Jersey, and received an English degree from St. Lawrence University. Following college he worked at a New York City literary agency for two years and then launched his writing career. To support himself while writing, he has worked as a taxi driver, a shipping clerk, and a house painter. Mr. Kent has had a lifelong interest in American history. Studying the U.S. presidents was his childhood hobby. His collection of presidential items includes books, pictures, and games, as well as several autographed letters.